**NATIONAL GEOGRAPHIC**

School Publishing

W9-ATA-985

# Our Government

## Ashley Hewitt

## PICTURE CREDITS

Cover, 2, 4 (right below), 5, 8, 11, 14 (above), 18, 19 (left below),
Photolibrary.com; 1, 21 (below), Jeff Greenberg/PhotoEdit; 4 (left above),
7 (left above), 12, 13 (below), 17 (left), 20 (right above), Getty Images;
4 (left below), Tony Freeman/PhotoEdit; 4 (right above), 6, 9 (right),
13 (left above), 13 (right above), 16 (left), 16 (right), 19 (left above);
20 (right below), APL/Corbis; 7 (left below), David Gordon/Alamy; 7 (right);
Visions of America, LLC/Alamy; 9 (left), Bob Daemmrich/PhotoEdit;
14 (below), JG Photography/Alamy; 15 (left) Dennis Hallinan/Alamy;
15 (right), kolvenbach/Alamy; 17 (right), Morguefile.com; 19 (right)
Michael Newman/PhotoEdit; 20 (left), Robert Brenner/PhotoEdit;
21 (above), Dennis MacDonald/PhotoEdit.

Produced through the worldwide resources of the National Geographic Society,
John M. Fahey, Jr., President and Chief Executive Officer; Gilbert M. Grosvenor,
Chairman of the Board; Nina D. Hoffman, Executive Vice President and
President, Books and Education Publishing Group.

## PREPARED BY NATIONAL GEOGRAPHIC SCHOOL PUBLISHING

Steve Mico, Executive Vice President and Publisher, Children's Books and
Education Publishing Group; Marianne Hiland, Editor in Chief; Lynnette Brent,
Executive Editors; Michael Murphy and Barbara Wood, Senior Editors; Nicole
Rouse, Editor; Bea Jackson, Design Director; David Dumo, Art Director; Shanin
Glenn, Designer; Margaret Sidlosky, Illustrations Director; Matt Wascavage,
Manager of Publishing Services; Sean Philpotts, Production Manager.

## MANUFACTURING AND QUALITY MANAGEMENT

Christopher A. Liedel, Chief Financial Officer; Phillip L. Schlosser, Vice
President; Clifton M. Brown III, Director.

## BOOK DEVELOPMENT

Ibis for Kids Australia Pty Limited.

Copyright © 2006 National Geographic Society. All rights reserved.
Reproduction of the whole or any part of the contents without written
permission from the publisher is prohibited. National Geographic, National
Geographic *Windows on Literacy*, and the Yellow Border are registered
trademarks of the National Geographic Society.

Published by the National Geographic Society
1145 17th Street, N.W.
Washington, D.C. 20036-4688

Product No. 4W1005066

ISBN-13: 978-1-4263-5062-7
ISBN-10: 1-4263-5062-7

2010 2009 2008
2 3 4 5 6 7 8 9 10 11 12 13 14 15

Printed in China

# Contents

# Think and Discuss

vote

2008 2020

VOTE HERE
VOTE HERE
2008
2020

obey the law

STOP

4

# What do you know about the U.S. government? How do people and government work together?

government leaders

White House

U.S. Capitol Building

# What Is Government?

The **government** is the group of people who run a country. The government makes **laws**. It keeps people safe. It also provides services.

Government leaders follow the Constitution. They also make decisions for our country.

Police officers, fire fighters, and sheriffs help keep people and communities safe.

Trash collection is a service that the government provides.

The United States Constitution describes how our government should work. It was written in 1787.

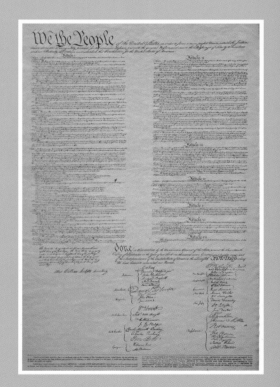

# Rights and Responsibilities

A **citizen** is a member of a country. Citizens have **rights**, or **freedoms**. They also have **responsibilities**. One responsibility is to respect the rights of others.

People follow rules so that everyone can be safe.

Citizens have the right to **vote**. They vote for leaders to run the government.

Freedom of speech is an important right. It means that people can talk and write about what they think and believe.

# Levels of Government

There are different levels of government in the United States. Each level of government is responsible for different things.

Washington, D.C.

**Federal**
The federal government is located in Washington, D.C., the capital of our country. It makes decisions for the whole country.

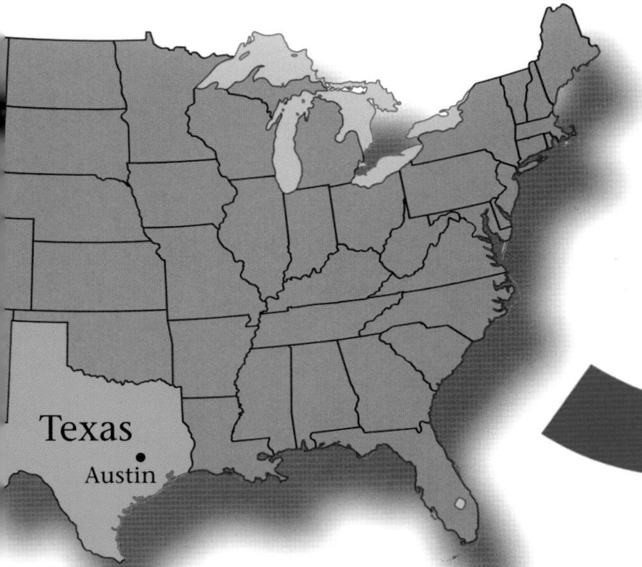

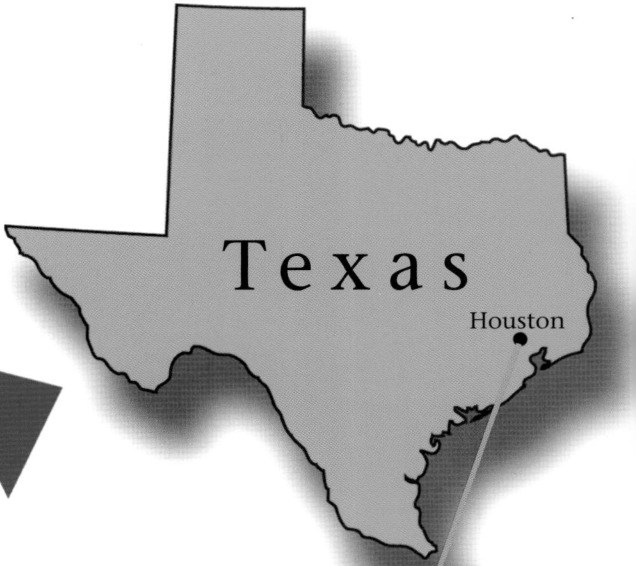

Texas

Houston

### State

There are 50 states in our country. Each has a state government. The state government is located in the capital city. The capital of Texas is Austin.

Texas

Austin

### Local

Each state has many local governments. They make decisions for their communities.

# Federal Government

The federal government is responsible for the whole country. It takes care of our people and land. It works with other countries.

The federal government runs the U.S. Mint. This is where our money is printed.

The armed forces are part of the federal government.

12

Government leaders work with other countries to make important decisions.

The Coast Guard protects our country's borders.

13

The federal government has three branches, or parts. Each branch has a job to do.

**The Legislative Branch**
The legislative branch, or Congress, meets in the Capitol building. It makes our country's laws.

### The Executive Branch
The **President** leads this branch and lives in the White House. This branch sees that laws are obeyed.

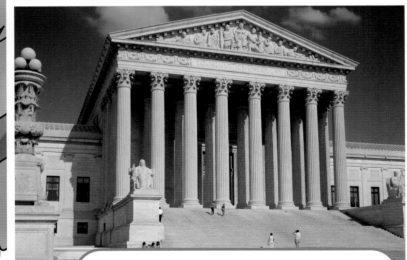

### The Judicial Branch
The Supreme Court leads the judicial branch. It meets in this building. This branch makes sure that laws are fair.

George Washington was the first President of the United States. He was President from 1789 to 1797.

Our capital city, Washington, D.C., was named after George Washington. He is also honored on the one dollar bill, which has his picture.

# State Government

There are fifty states in our country. Each state has its own government. State governments are responsible for many things.

State highway patrol officers make sure that people obey traffic laws.

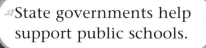
State governments help support public schools.

The flag is a **symbol** of our country. A symbol is something that stands for something else.

Our flag has fifty white stars, one for each state. It has thirteen red and white stripes. The stripes represent the thirteen colonies that started our country. The first flag had only thirteen stars. There was one star for each of the thirteen colonies.

Rangers look after state parks and teach people about the environment.

17

# Local Government

Communities, such as cities and towns, also have governments. These local governments have responsibilities, too.

Fire fighters work for local fire departments to put out fires.

Local governments provide money for libraries.

Many local governments collect trash and recycling.

Many cities and local governments have a mayor. Some cities also have a city council. The mayor works with the city council to make laws and solve problems.

19

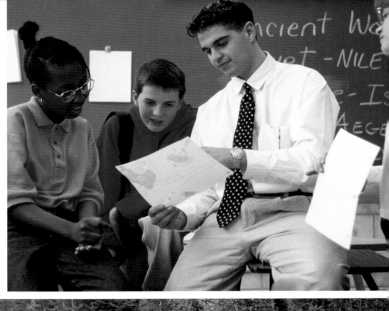

LOCATOR TRAIL

# What does government do?
# What rights and responsibilities do citizens have?

citizen

freedom

government

responsibilty

right

symbol

vote

# Glossary

KEY CONCEPT

**citizen** (page 8)
A person who is a member of a country
Citizens of the United States have the right to vote.

KEY CONCEPT

**freedom** (page 8)
Being allowed to do, say, and live as you choose
People have the freedom to say what they think.

KEY CONCEPT

**government** (page 6)
The group of people who run a country
The government does many different things.

**law** (page 6)
A rule that everyone must obey
A driver who stops at a stop sign is following the law.

**President** (page 15)
The leader of the executive branch of the U.S. government
The President lives in the White House.

KEY CONCEPT

**responsibility** (page 8)
Something that a person must do or take care of
Taking care of the environment is a responsibility.

KEY CONCEPT

**right** (page 8)
Something that is due to a person
All citizens have the right to education.

KEY CONCEPT

**symbol** (page 17)
Something that represents something else
The American flag is a symbol of the United States.

KEY CONCEPT

**vote** (page 9)
To chose between two or more options
People vote for leaders to run the government.

# Index